nature's friends

Frogs

by Ann Heinrichs

Content Adviser: Harold K. Voris, Curator of Amphibians and Reptiles, Field Museum of Natural History, Chicago, Illinois
Science Adviser: Terrence E. Young Jr., M.Ed., M.L.S., Jefferson Parish (La.) Public Schools
Reading Adviser: Dr. Linda D. Labbo, Department of Reading Education, College of Education, The University of Georgia

COMPASS POINT BOOKS
MINNEAPOLIS, MINNESOTA

The author wishes to thank Kate Griebler for her kind assistance.

Compass Point Books
3109 West 50th Street, #115
Minneapolis, MN 55410

Visit Compass Point Books on the Internet at *www.compasspointbooks.com*
or e-mail your request to *custserv@compasspointbooks.com*

Photographs ©: Digital Stock, cover, 1; Robert McCaw, 4–5, 10–11; Michael & Patricia Fogden/Corbis, 6–7; Cheryl A. Ertelt, 8–9; Joe McDonald, 12–13, 14–15, 18–19; Gary Meszaros/Visuals Unlimited, 16; Sally A. Morgan, Ecoscene/Corbis, 20; Dwight Kuhn, 23; DigitalVision, 24–25; Ronnie Kaufman/Corbis, 26–27.

Editors: E. Russell Primm, Emily J. Dolbear, Pam Rosenberg, and Patricia Stockland
Photo Researcher: Svetlana Zhurkina
Photo Selector: Linda S. Koutris
Designer: The Design Lab

Library of Congress Cataloging-in-Publication Data
Heinrichs, Ann.
  Frogs / by Ann Heinrichs.
    p. cm. — (Nature's friends)
  Summary: Introduces the physical characteristics, methods of movement, habitats, feeding habits, life cycles, and different types of frogs.
  Includes bibliographical references (p.   ).
  ISBN 0-7565-0436-8 (hardcover)
  1. Frogs—Juvenile literature. [1. Frogs.] I. Title.
  QL668.E2 H4125 2003
  597.8'9—dc21   2002009936

Table of Contents

NOTE: In this book, words that are defined in the glossary are in **bold** *the first time they appear in the text.*

Frogs Are Fun!

Ribbit! Ribbit! A frog croaks. *Splash!* A frog hops into a pond.

It's fun to watch frogs hopping. Frogs live all around us. We don't always see them, but we hear them croaking. They gather in woods or near ponds. Soon their "songs" fill the air.

Long ago, people believed that frogs were magic. They said frogs could bring rain or good luck. One tale tells about a frog prince. A princess kisses the frog. Then he changes into a handsome prince.

Frogs are not really magic. They do help us in many ways, though. Let's get to know our frog friends!

Frogs are not magic, but they can be very helpful to humans!

What Is a Frog?

A frog is an amphibian. Amphibians begin their life in water as **larvae.** Later they usually live near water. Frogs are **cold-blooded** animals. Their blood is not really cold. Their body is the same temperature as the air or water around them.

The world's biggest frog is Africa's goliath frog. It grows up to 1 foot (30 centimeters) long. The tiny gold frog of Brazil is the smallest frog in the **southern hemisphere.** Adult gold frogs are only about 10 millimeters long. That's about three-eighths of an inch.

The smallest frog in the **northern hemisphere** was discovered in 1996. It doesn't have a common name yet. It is about the same size as the gold frog. Each of these frogs would fit on your thumbnail!

This little gold frog is one of the smallest frogs in the world. ▶

Where Frogs Live

Frogs have lived on Earth for more than 200 million years. They were here even before some dinosaurs! Today, frogs live almost everywhere in the world. Hot, wet regions—known as the tropics—have the most frogs. None live on icy Antarctica.

Frogs like to live in wet areas. Some live in woods with plenty of wet leaves where they can hide. Some frogs live in trees. Their toe pads work like suction cups. They can cling to branches, leaves, and other smooth surfaces. Some frogs even burrow into wet ground. Their "fingers" are like claws.

Many frogs are good swimmers. Their webbed back feet help them swim. However, some frogs will drown if they can't get to land.

The toe pads of this red-eyed treefrog help it cling to surfaces.

How Frogs Are Built

Frogs are vertebrates. That means they have a backbone. A frog's back legs are long and strong. It's two front legs are short.

Frogs have big eyes that bulge out. They can see in almost every direction. Behind each eye is a disk. It's an eardrum for hearing sounds.

Frogs breathe through their **nostrils.** The air goes into their lungs. Their skin "breathes," too. In the water, a frog gets **oxygen** through its skin.

A frog's heart pumps blood through its body. Its stomach and intestines digest food.

Frogs use their skin and their noses to breathe. ▶

Frogs and Their Skin

Did you ever hold a frog? Its skin may have felt wet. A frog's skin oozes **mucus.** The mucus keeps the skin soft and wet. A frog's skin is very important for it to live.

Frogs get air and water through their skin. They must keep their skin healthy. So they keep shedding their old skin. Some frogs shed their skin every few days.

Think about how you pull off your sweater. That's how frogs pull off their old skin. They pull it over their head. Then some frogs eat the skin!

The skin of frogs often looks wet.

Jumping Like a Frog

How tall are you? Let's say you are about 50 inches (127 centimeters) tall. Now let's say you are a frog. If you were a frog, and you were that tall, you could jump more than 1,000 inches (2,540 centimeters). That's more than 83 feet (25 meters). It's almost as far as home plate to first base!

Frogs can jump more than twenty times their length. A South African frog set the world jumping record. It jumped more than 33 feet (10 meters).

A green frog leaps through the air. ▶

How Frogs Eat

Stick out your tongue. As you can see, it's attached to the back of your mouth. A frog's tongue is attached to the front of its mouth. It folds up inside the mouth.

Along comes a juicy bug. The tongue unfolds in a flash. It shoots out and catches the bug. The tongue is sticky, so the bug sticks to it.

Most frogs eat insects. They swallow insects whole. Then their eyes sink in. The frog's eyes help push the food down its throat!

Frogs must have water. They do not drink, however. They take in water through their skin.

◀ *This leopard frog is getting ready to swallow a dragonfly.*

Ribbit! Ribbit!

Both male and female frogs can croak. Only male frogs, however, can "sing," or make loud calls. They do it to attract female mates. Sometimes they do it to keep other males away. Other times, frogs croak to say it's going to rain.

How do frogs croak? They force air past their vocal cords. Most males also have a vocal sac. A vocal sac is a bag of skin around the throat. They puff up the sac to make a loud call. This call can be heard far away.

Tiny frogs may make chirping sounds. You can make this sound, too. Just get a comb. Then run your fingernail across the tips of its teeth.

Male frogs puff up their vocal sacs to make loud croaks. ▶

Mating and Reproducing

At mating time, a male green frog hops into the water. He begins to "sing." Soon a female jumps into the water. She lays a clump of eggs. Some frogs lay thousands of eggs at once.

The male holds on to the female's back. As the eggs come out, he spreads sperm on them. This fertilizes the eggs so they can develop. In one to three weeks, the eggs hatch. Out come little tadpoles. They are frog larvae.

◄ *Frog eggs*

Growing Up

Tadpoles look sort of like fish. They have plump bodies and long tails. Like fish, they breathe through **gills.** They eat algae and other water plants. Most frog parents do nothing to care for their young.

The tadpoles' eyes and mouths get bigger. Their tails get shorter and shorter. They grow lungs for breathing air. Their heart, bones, and other parts grow. They begin to grow legs. Soon they are ready for life on land.

This tadpole has grown legs but has not completely lost its tail. ▶

Keeping Safe

Snakes like to eat frogs. Some birds and fish eat frogs, too. Frogs' colors often match or blend in with their setting. That helps them hide from danger. Some frogs are brown or black. They blend in with bark and dead leaves. Many tree frogs are green, like healthy leaves.

Some frogs are bright red, orange, or blue. The skin of these frogs often holds poison. Their bright colors warn enemies to stay away.

This brightly colored poison arrow frog has poisonous skin.

Frogs Are Our Friends!

Not all frogs are alike. There are many different kinds of frogs. They live in many different places around the world. We are lucky to have all kinds of frogs around. Frogs eat mosquitoes that bite people. They eat insects that harm plants.

Frogs are helpful to scientists, too. Scientists study frogs to learn how frogs' bodies work. They also test human medicines on frogs. Some frogs' bodies produce medicines. These medicines can treat human **diseases.**

Some kinds of frogs are dying out. They may get sick from dirty air and water. Others may have nowhere to live. Their woods and ponds are disappearing. Let's help protect our friends the frogs!

It can be fun to learn more about frogs. ▶

Glossary

cold-blooded—having a body temperature that changes with the temperature of the surroundings

diseases—illnesses

gills—organs that allow an animal to get oxygen from water

larvae—animals that recently hatched from eggs and do not look like their parents

mucus—a slippery fluid that coats and protects a body part

oxygen—a gas found in air

nostrils—openings in the nose through which animals take in air

northern hemisphere—the part of Earth that is north of the equator

southern hemisphere—the part of Earth that is south of the equator

Let's Look at True Frogs

Class: Amphibian
Order: Anura
Family: Ranidae

Range: True frogs can be found on all continents except Antarctica. They make their homes on or near water.

Life span: Life spans can vary depending on the species of frog. Most frogs in the wild live for at least two years. Some species can live much longer.

Life stages: Adult frogs lay eggs, usually in or near water. In three to twenty-five days, the eggs hatch and tadpoles come out. The length of time it takes for eggs to hatch depends on the kind of frog. Also, the water temperature may help decide hatching time. A tadpole can take from ten days to more than two years to develop into an adult frog. The length of time it takes depends on the species.

Food: Adult frogs eat insects. Sometimes they eat spiders, earthworms, and minnows. Tadpoles usually eat algae and other plant matter.

Did You Know?

A marsupial frog carries her eggs in a pouch, like a kangaroo. What does she do when the eggs hatch into tadpoles? She uses her toes to open the pouch. Then she spills the tadpoles into the water.

Barking frogs live in Texas. They are called barking frogs because their voices sound like the barking of small dogs.

The frog is sometimes called an indicator species. This means that the frog is one of the first kinds of animals to be harmed by changes in our environment. Scientists are worried about the decrease in the number of frogs in the world. Some think it is a sign that Earth may be less able to support life.

The North American wood frog survives the winter by going into a deep hibernation. Its breathing and heartbeat stop. Up to 65 percent of the water in its body turns to ice. When the weather warms up in the spring, the frog thaws out and goes about its daily life.

Junior Herpetologists

Herpetologists are scientists who study amphibians and reptiles. You can be a herpetologist, too! You will need a notebook, a pen or pencil, and a fishing net. Find a pond. Look for frogs in or near the pond. When you see a frog, spend a few minutes watching it. Write down a description of the frog. Then, carefully scoop up the frog in your net. Gently pick up the frog. Make some observations about its size and how its skin feels. When you are finished, carefully put the frog back where you found it. Repeat this process with two more frogs.

After observing the frogs, try to answer these questions:
What color was each frog?
About how big was each frog?
How did the frogs' skin feel?
What kinds of things did you see the frogs doing?
Did all three frogs look the same?
    If not, what was different about them?
Do you think that the frogs were all from the same species?
    Why or why not?
Draw a picture of a frog.

Want to Know More?

AT THE LIBRARY

Arnosky, Jim. *All About Frogs.* New York: Scholastic, 2002.

Greenaway, Theresa, Chris Fairclough (illustrator), Colin Newman (illustator), and Stefan Chabluk (photographer). *Tadpoles.* Austin, Tex.: Raintree/Steck-Vaughn, 2000.

Kottke, Jan. *From Tadpole to Frog.* Danbury, Conn.: Children's Press, 2000.

ON THE WEB

Frogs

http://www.pca.state.mn.us/kids/frogsforkids.html

For pictures of frogs, frog calls, coloring pages, and information about frogs

Frogs

http://www.exploratorium.edu/frogs/

For a lot of information about frogs, including frog myths from many cultures

THROUGH THE MAIL

Frogwatch USA Coordinator

National Wildlife Federation

1400 16th Street, N.W.

Suite 501

Washington, DC 20036

202/797-6891

To write for information about the Frogwatch program

ON THE ROAD

American Museum of Natural History

Central Park West at 79th Street

New York, NY 10024-5192

212/769-5100

To visit the Spectrum of Life exhibit and learn how frogs are related to other living things

The Field Museum

1400 S. Lake Shore Drive

Chicago, IL 60605

312/922-9410

To visit the Reptiles and Amphibians exhibit

Index

About the Author: Ann Heinrichs grew up in Fort Smith, Arkansas. She began playing the piano at age three and thought she would grow up to be a pianist. Instead, she became a writer. Now she has written more than eighty books for children and young adults. Several of her books have won national awards. Ms. Heinrichs now lives in Chicago, Illinois. She enjoys martial arts and traveling to faraway countries.